Here, Dale Booton bestows us with poems both dexterous and endearing, weaving together affinities into a tapestry of queer camaraderie – of nights becoming day, their introspection. Voices and bodies converge, enraptured or in longing 'to abandon / what came before'. In reading On This Stretch of Queerland, *it is felt that, as Booton's speaker puts it: 'the weight of the words is in his soul'.*

Peter Scalpello

Alert to the subtlest flavours of desire, these skilful poems probe 'unattached silence' and 'the taste of your name'. In a century packed with 'phantom vibrations' and 'passing meteorites', their speakers urgently comb night clubs, phone screens, and bedroom conversations for a gate that leads to transcendence and makes 'the body a vessel / of untapped weightlessness'.

John McCullough

First published in 2024 by Fourteen Publishing.
fourteenpoems.com

Design and typeset by Stromberg Design.
strombergdesign.co.uk

Proofreading and copy editing by Lara Kavanagh.
lk-copy.com

Printed by Print2Demand Ltd, Westoning, Bedfordshire, UK.

Dale Booton has asserted their right to be identified as the author of this work in accordance with the Copyright, Designs and Patents Act 1988.

This book is sold subject to the conditions that it shall not be lent, resold, hired out or otherwise circulated without the publisher's prior consent. Any republishing of the individual works must be agreed in advance.

ISBN:
978-1-7391697-9-4

ON THIS STRETCH OF QUEERLAND

Dale Booton

For Luke, Darren, and Mike.

Time, like love, cannot be held.

contents:

My Lover Reads Poetry for the First Time 8
His Shadow is Not Mine 9
The Night Swallows all Sorts of Mischief 11
Ephemera 12
We Kiss Beneath Suffolk Street Queensway 13
Dining Out 15
That's the Part I Love Most 16
Boyfriends 17
In the Cinema 18
Over 19
Nightclub 20
Don't Crawl 21
Night Owl 22
He Asks Me to Kiss Him 23
Thirteen Ways of Looking at Grindr 24
Summer of Love 27
My History Walks the Floor 28
On Skating the First Lap 29
Wanderer 30
Host 31
Brain Too Wired and Everywhere 32
I Think of All the Drunken Nights 33
Foreskin 34
The Stone 35
Take Me Home 36
Like the Sun & the Moon 37
Faggot 38
Saturday Night in the Village Inn 39

Acknowledgements 40

My Lover Reads Poetry for the First Time

he begins with application   stops
asks *wait so why*
has the poet gone onto a new line
here what's that about

I try to explain emphasis   the honour
of something holding value
of speed and rhythm
that natural flow of thought

how do I read the poem   I smile
make a stupid comment
about using his eyes   tell him
the weight of the words is in his soul

His Shadow is Not Mine

yet I cast it   stand in it
        like I am the centre of its universe
                & the strobe lights are just
                        passing meteorites   not the eyes

            of those he could be/has been
    with   the wall is a black hole
dragging me   & the bar
    is another system

        with its own planets

           & I must
        be a comet
    touring cosmos after cosmos

like home is a place that can
      be found   or perhaps

        deep space is just a refuge of men
          somewhere to linger

        until the light from the nearest star
    hits   offers a warm touch
or inclination to orbit
    in the vacuum of the club

        pull me closer/please

          & his density
    is an entire constellation burning up

    until the galaxy is no more

& I am left

    in total eclipse

The Night Swallows All Sorts of Mischief

another light has come on you tell me about it over the phone while Bliss yaps at your side I picture you half-holding her half-trying to concentrate on your words *alright titty-bit it's just a light* the curtains are usually closed by half-seven but the fireworks have been clawing at each of the week's nights the dog is scared but it slightly lessens it for her to see what is making the bright chaotic snarling she cautiously watches the sharp shoots of red merging into blue into green into blackness like watching a snail retreat into its shell she yelps drags herself over her paws before jolting back you tell me this in your own way trying to find the best descriptors because *you're an English teacher I can't be saying the wrong things now* I scoff and you tell me of the neighbour's boy who has been trying to hop fences *he's sliced his leg open on the council flat spike daft sod with nothing better to do they took all the little clubs for them bloody government like the one you used to do aikido at* I agree you ask of my night while I stand outside the nearest gay bar to home I tell you *yeah yeah i'm all good* watch two men eat each other's faces as the bloodshot eyes of a woman appear in the gap of the door *when are you round next* I tell you *tomorrow you're a good lad* silent moment *you out tonight* I lie tell you i'm just walking home *late night cinema trip* the bar door opens a bearded man steps out to smoke rolls up lights takes a drag question yeah it was good fireworks explode in the near distance over a building set to be demolished the sort of foreboding I teach *well I'll see you tomorrow then* his eyes drift up to the discoball moon linger like a musked touch from a loved one you haven't seen in so long he exhales streams of darkroom starlight his contemplation falls I catch it *yeah I'll see you tomorrow around midday* he takes a long drag his gaze a rushing warmth as he takes another drag *yeah see you tomorrow love you* I repeat hang up imagine myself curled between his smoke-filled lips

Ephemera

we deconstruct ourselves in snappy messages
between the ogles
of each other's pictures

decode thought and feeling through gay-panic
emoji-flirtation
does he really like me or-

thirty minutes without response   fumbling thumbs
phantom vibrations
beside the plug socket

unattached silence   moon a fetid ball of doubt
this is so much
of nothing   punishing night

ping   finally   the restoration of the morning sun
in my room
I build some version of you

We Kiss Beneath Suffolk Street Queensway

the moon is a giant *naru* against the *kalo jam* sky
the stars like coconut sheddings

I stare into your *panuta* eyes
and realise I have not tasted joy like this
in so long

                         and I speak of such sweet things
because kissing you reminds me of
that childish excitement at the pick n' mix counter

and quickly I realise that I could want too much of you
too soon   that my hunger

                                     is not a devouring
but a relentless craving to pick you
apart

         to savour each morsel
like I have so rarely done before   always too quick
to harvest every bite

                       but you are more
than a celebratory treat   more than a Michelin meal
in some suave London restaurant

I cannot afford

I have consumed so many unready fruits
have spat out the hostility
                                     of their emaciated seeds
washed out the sourness of their stay
                                         with gin

but tonight
you have cleansed
my palate
                              tonight
I would sooner starve
than feast on the honeyed spirit
        of your flesh

Dining Out

you introduce me to your favourite Chinese food
double fried chicken doused in chillies
and my throat flares at the sight of them   lips already crying out
for water   you grin   watch my face   chopsticks
poised like the front legs of a praying mantis
I strike   snatch up a fair amount   toss it into the trembling
abyss   while chewing   I focus on your face
coke-glass eyes   night-framed glasses   nosey tongue
try to distract myself from the napalm spice
dare not look towards the oasis of water
a fork away   *what do you think*   and my voice
tries to battle its way through the flames   wants to tell you
that there is no taste like the taste of your name
in my mouth   but instead falters at *it's nice but a bit hot   for me*

That's the Part I love Most

when you stay   and after
the sheets remain unchanged for days   made
and unmade by the rushing tenure
of your husk

I wake up wanting to touch you   reach
into the besideme space filled
with absence   the hollowness
like a blanket

drag it over me   myself
in the memory of your body   there
imagine us in the years
to come

once staying became stayed
and the flesh once smooth has creased
like sheets   washed and re-washed
in your scent

Boyfriends

you had said it
in a way
I felt I misheard you   or feared
it was a joke

that's why I didn't speak
made it
uncomfortable
my side-eye glances like paper cuts

salty silence
in the wound
my voice drowning
arms flailing   hoping for shore

we kept afloat
in the theatre
my hand on your knee
comfort reminder

caught
in the tide of my mind
I waited
until the long walk back

tip-toed beside you
throat dry
words stumbling
like a drunk over the pavement

it spewed out
chunks of hope   pieces of fear
you held my hair   said
don't worry   I've got you

In the Cinema

you drop my hand
ovenfresh Pyrex

it shatters
on impact   faux leather

armrest catches
the pieces of me

do I make
a sound   do you

hear it
over the footfalls

of eyes
how quickly they move

we sit in silence
the movie a troubled relationship

where love
is a bond that can kill

and pain
now motivation to live

I sweep myself up
as the credits roll

leaps of faith
from a cliff edge

I have never
learned to swim

Over

the sun
is a giant blister

it pops
swells out the night

its longing
a thick matting

of pus
and glistening shame

like freckles against
the salted

run-off skin
rough

as mondays
damp as starlight

Nightclub

I have heard the music speak to me
it was the bodies of friends and strangers
that introduced us   kindred arms wrapped
around the uncomfortable   *relax*
we move as one
there is strength in physicality
there is softness in letting go
that not-so-sober shove onto the dancefloor
that not-so-innocent rush to be close to some other
proximity is breath
a closely guarded secret
here my voice is not foreign   this place
where love and lust are two words
that begin with l   like living

Don't Crawl

into the outdoor light of the smoking area
you mightn't like what you see
once the veil has been lifted   that
club commodity of dry ice
obscurer to the drunken kisses
and doe-eyed glances into the headlights
of desire   if you can call it that
that which dwells within the damp drum
music on shuffle   DJ offering odd details missed
by vodka-soaked hearing   body swagger
to the beat of boozed breath
lights down   that taste of darkness
it lingers   even as you stagger home   burger
in hand   dawn peering from behind pintglass clouds

Night Owl

against the backdrop of slutdrops
you shuffle from left to right   arms antenna

registered awkwardness from sombre sober nights
single glass of coke with ice   watch

the bark-eyed men wriggle from their t-shirts
hark trousers up to calves   their skin

glistening from sweat and joy and unaware
of the morning toilet bowl sufferings   it is

so much like the weather   of how the rain is always
coming   but not yet   maybe

they burn like the sun   hoisting themselves
into the centre of their own universes

the twinkling strobe-light eyes
of men who want to fuck them raw   and rough

like the end of the night as you gather them
up like sheep   herd them into taxis   friends' arms

and front doors   tell them you'll wait up
do they know how much you care for them

do they thank you when you pick them up
from the chippy   the street corner   the backstreet alley

He Asks Me to Kiss Him

but I don't know how long he's been out
I just got here   his fingers
tease a trail
down my arm to my palm
where he waits   eyes like open
bedroom windows
after having snuck out
they call to me
climb in

but I don't know how to tell him I can't
so I just smile   reach in
for a hug
his body a hot water bottle
on a winter's night   blanket
pulled up tight
sofa snuggles   why
does he plead
come on

but I don't know how to not kiss him
and he's there   lips red
with hunger
or thirst for more than
a glass   I could be a fountain
so I nuzzle
past his neck to a
cheek flushed
have me

Thirteen Ways of Looking at Grindr

i
~~hey how are you? how was your~~
~~day? what are you interested in?~~
hey horny?

ii
I scroll the message tab
those blue building bricks of conversation
I asked for an extension
but it's just more space
for the cold to linger

iii
single lookin 4 fun friends & dates
all you can eat buffet
I hunger for none

iv
before silence
that jack-in-the-box mating call

note to self
turn notifications off

v
orange and black echoes
of energy and optimism
in a mask we carry
on silent deep in pockets
who is that we are hiding from

vi
ourselves in the mirror
body bare slab
Y incision by eyes

on the other side
of some other screen

little green dot vanishes
online 7 minutes ago

vii
o lover stretch my heart
like you want to climb inside it
drive my body down
whatever nameless motorway
you choose

viii
I have known men
boulderous in their refrain
heart dwelling
within a cave that won't even hold
the dark

ix
how lonely the drowning night
how silent
its gargled cry for help

x
vestiges of *accom don't travel*
lay as Berlin wall souvenirs

we release into the world some part
of ourselves
expecting to be freed

xi
he rode me until his body
could take no more

puddled on my chest
the salted sweat of our love
no
effort
in the air like the way dust settles
waits to be wiped away

xii
masc 4 masc
have a face pic don't respond to taps

xiii
evening grew from afternoon
it has rained and now I watch
the moon search for stars
tears falling as voice notes
where have they all gone

Summer of Love

I'm reminded of a promise
your t-shirt in my waistband
your eyes to the ceiling
arms spread like history

speakers guide you to freedom
the body a vessel of
untapped weightlessness

I am your protector   sworn
defender of the drunken arts
tender endurance of the night
you lay upon the dancefloor

flashing lights as forgotten
moments   our time
small globes we mistake for eyes

My History Walks the Floor

like a nightclub   bustling with bodies
and faces slurred by groans

names spilled over floors
left until morning   when sun

breaks through uncurtained glass
dries up what damp remains

there is a listlessness
in waiting   letting the body fall

to disregard   allowing some other
to become no other then

no one   that turn of the tide
as emptiness carries back to the shore

the shell of a good time   retreats
coverts in the corner

of the bar   orders a double
waits for taste to be more than momentary

On Skating the First Lap

      I hold
      your boyfriend's
      hand

stumble
into confidence
lights murk
the natural circuit

      anti-clockwork
      efforts scored
      into cold terrain

you push me
gloved hands
a harness
around my waist

      I breathe
      let the chilled air
      soothe me

families
and couples
stagger stumble
blue feet amiss

      ricochet
      laughter like
      a game of squash

here on the ice
there is
freedom
in enclosure

Wanderer

                    I have travelled
the length of this country
looking for somewhere   your touch
is the closest thing to home
I have not felt renovation like this in so long
the cracks and creaks of my body
have been afraid to be loved   but here
my legs are planted and my arms are motorways
heading to you

                    where so many
have drowned   our mouths are a bridge
between cities   what walks between our tongues
is not familiarity but community
or at least that sense of sameness
in this place where faces are skimmed stones
hands clawing at banks in search
of a safe space for the stomach to abandon
what came before

Host

of my own body
I hold a celebration
of openness
and guests arrive
with
their own intentions
leave their own mark
like owning
some microscopic
part of me
or owning
the text
that comes two weeks later
that week-long course
of amoxicillin
or that ceftriaxone needle
in the ass
body owned
by empire
of fast-fading love
of toxic fragility
willingness to please
another
ownership
of the broken
of the impotent
and the vexed
of offers
never truly granted

Brain Too Wired and Everywhere

it wasn't funny before
waiting for a taxi while O pissed
in the street   called out men
like it was an auction

but on the sofa
the music is a slutdropping rainbow
and friends are deep in convos
with tears about their fears

age and jobs and failures
and he tries not to pass out
of himself   watches glass realms
like the declare of an ocean

his voice a hallelujah
of shits and giggles   pastures
of days before he knew
manufactured alleviation

I Think of All the Drunken Nights

we've managed
to carry
each other
home
moon dimmed
by sambuca shots
and corner
sniffs from
blacked-out bottle
much of ourselves
is stemmed
from bodies reaching
to music
beyond lyric
and beat
mechanism
of movement
flushing
out of us
like an escape
that rush
to be closer
to something
that
cannot be
touched

Foreskin

pulled   stretched   yanked back
foreskin of my best friend
lacking foreskin of my best friend's boyfriend
who praises my foreskin
with his tongue   like a hood
he can hide in   the world too bright
how I had with the foreskins
of strangers and friends and boyfriends
his boyfriend   like the foreskin
that looked like a bin bag
inside what looked like off-meat
or shoved beneath the cubicle gap
foreskin I wouldn't touch with my mouth
if you paid me   texture not quite
foreskin enough   but like clingfilm
or plastic melting   shiny
with pre-cum or spit   the taste
of unstressed flesh   the dried or undried
dribbles of piss   foreskin of Tina's ex-boyfriend
when she said she couldn't understand
its purpose   that it was as pointless
as the man it belonged to
as if the skin had been foretold
to remember the shape of limited use

The Stone

I found it after you left
on the sofa where we had sat
for hours   our voices
like raindrops from leaf
into stream   I pocketed it
forgot about it   let it sit
in my jeans for days
taught my lessons
bought my groceries
drank tea in my favourite café
ate those microwave meals
the nights can get so empty
only felt it the next time
we met   a sudden
scratch   I winced and you
asked what was wrong
I said nothing
or nothing
I cannot recall which now
but the following week
you invited me
to dinner   your boyfriend said
people in glass houses
I felt smashed
pocket torn like moonlight
roughness rounded
by a gentle caress
or the side-eye shuffle
down Hurst st
slabs struck with an acuteness
littered
with all that has been
thrown away

Take Me Home

rain visits us like bouncers
hurries us to the queue
beneath the nightclub shelter

inside swathes and drags
of arms like currents
hushed by gravelly charm

your eyes electric-brown
beneath the struggle
of lights trying to see

lips land I long to tread
despite ourselves we watch
vested-angels descend

Like the Sun & the Moon

we admire each other from afar
draw ourselves as perfect equals
amidst the vacant bleakness of
night   only you orbit another
& so often we almost touch
fingertips like comet streams
snatched away by the sight of
some other star   out there
there is that planet I see you
with   inseparable claim to
forever floating pair   & yet
you drift   like debris from
heartbroken supernova   & I
wonder how long I have until
I become that empty black hole

Faggot

in form of boy / in form of / man / moonlit dp / listens / to the others / bitching glory / like it's the second coming / and coming / like it's the last time they ever will / over themselves / others / their names / now with fag emojis / like this is fag life / all / online / smashing tweets against / one another / like this / is a bar fight / and there is only one / way to live / the swing song of Newton's cradle / by blue ticks / and no / ticks / chiselled jawline / and flab / and beard / and face smooth like a young twink's / not yet ripened into / glow / hosts of summerbody ready / thirst traps / and wet mouths / and head / leaking pre / come / see / how they say that word / is / offensive / like / we don't own it / can't / own it / like / we / can't own anything / and I have hated / myself / and / the word / and myself with / the word / the way most / do / have tasted its bitterness / across my face / like lashes / on the tip / of my tongue / have spat / the word at myself / in the mirror / the way a man in a car did / at speed / like my reflection is / nothing / but word / smash it / think / shut up / you are more / than word / queer extraordinaire / grand inquisitor of vocab / echoing *yass queen* / and *werk* / like a runaway jock / who dresses for the gods and wants / nothing / more than to get fucked / in the ass / by peng strangers / loaded up / in the dark / then rush home to wash / to vomit / to rid yourself of them / butt cheeks flat / against the rim / squelched expulsion / of self-hatred / listen / I know an artist / painting us as colour / he is noun / is us / in flesh / and blood / and body / in whole / with thoughts / and / feelings / who knows us / and / does us / is done by us / in the dark / not strangers / but us / we are / not / strangers / come / here / and he can paint you / as family / as you / want / to be / as grey / straight / lines

Saturday Night in the Village Inn

it's that pitter-patter of copper   smiles drenched
in vodka coke   dancefloor beats
spreading out like streams to the hearingheart

that seminal rush of love or lust or whatever it is
the body can take   nostril flared
at the rim of the bottle   firework sensation

more drinks   bitter-lemonade eyes lurk the corner
sticky with spillages   quick glance
at the elephant in the room   last week's catch

beat change into festive cheer   deep breath taken
and *all I want*   arms around shoulders
waists   spurts of warm breath on earlobe

throbbing eardrum beneath the speaker at the DJ
booth   the lungs hold notes
the morningthroat feels calling for water

Acknowledgements

"That's the Part I love Most" was first published by Muswell Press in *Queer Life, Queer Love 2*.

"Night Owl" was first published by *Impossible Archetype*.

"Nightclub" was first published by *iamb*.

"Thirteen Ways of Looking at Grindr" is after Wallace Stevens' "Thirteen Ways of Looking at a Blackbird"

"Summer of Love" is for Darren.

"Foreskin" is after Keith Jarret's "I'll Give Thanks" from *Emerging from Matter* and was first published by & Change.

"The Stone" is after Kat Ryan's "Carrying a Ladder". It is for Luke.

"Faggot" is for Will Belshah and was first published by & Change.

"Saturday Night in the Village Inn" is for Mike.

Huge gratitude to Andrew McMillan, Piero Toto, Michael Symmons Roberts, Barbara Crossley, David Scott, Laura Strickland, Tom Lawlor, Melissa Manderson, Archisha Moudgil, and Marina Walton for their invaluable comments on many of these poems.

Thank you to my friends Luke, Darren, and Mike, without whom this pamphlet would not have taken form. They are a constant rock for me – and I wouldn't be me without them. I owe them so much for their constant encouragement, kindness, and love.

And, of course, a multitude of gratitude to Ben and *fourteen poems* for their belief in and efforts with my pamphlet. I am blessed for it to have found a home.